The Bond We Shared

Copyright © Geraldine Whitsett

ISBN: 978-1-958186-18-3

Publisher, Editor and Book Design:

Fiery Beacon Publishing House, LLC

Fiery Beacon Consulting and Publishing Group

Graphics: FBPH Graphics Team, Dashona Smith

The Bond We Shared

The Gift of Love

By

Geraldine Whitsett

Dedicated...

To Barbara Pilgrim who taught me how to love myself, how to share and how to forgive, and to Nettie Seaberry who provided continuous support and assistance to complete this book.

Table of Contents

Chapter 1

The Struggle

Born in a small town in North Carolina in1935, I remember at the age of five, wanting to be a teacher. The oldest of eight children I was always instructing my four sisters and three brothers. As the years passed, my mom told me that my dad only went to school for three full days of his life. I thought that was strange because he helped us with homework but she informed me that she graduated high school and taught him to read and write. I was determined to complete school with the understanding that if my father had completed his education, it would have enabled our entire family to prosper. That was motivation enough for me even if I didn't go to college.

After graduation I obtained a job, employed as a tray girl in a large hospital in Greensboro, North Carolina. "Tray Service" is a type of service that does not use the regular usual dining table, but instead dishes are prepared and arranged in trays, which are then brought to the patient. This service was used to serve patients in the hospitals in Greensboro.

After a few months, the supervisor found out that I was good at decoding the color slips on trays given to patients and assigned me to the second floor at the hospital because it had the largest number of patients. During this time of course my pay increased. Checking my savings account, I realized that I had saved enough money to enroll in college for at least one semester. I applied to North Carolina Agricultural and Technical University; A&T was famous for its engineering program. I was accepted to the School of Institutional Management.

I attended (A&T) College for two years before dropping out for financial reasons, but not before I participated in the lunch counter sit-in at the Woolworth's discount department store in Greensboro. Back then, Woolworth's allowed Blacks to shop, but they weren't allowed to eat at the lunch counter. It was February 1960 when I answered a call for participants from flyers advertised around the campus. Within weeks the protests spread to all the Woolworth's throughout the south and by July 1960 the Woolworth chain agreed to desegregate their lunch counters. I hadn't realized at the time that I was part of a historical moment, but without a doubt, I realize it now.

Attending classes made it hard to continue working at the hospital because of the hours. I worked eight hours daily then trying to complete the assigned reports from my professors, was more than I anticipated and it became harder to concentrate on school and my course workload. I began seeking other places of employment and answered several advertisements in daily newspapers in the area and applied; little did I know that one of the jobs was for the day care offered on campus. I applied and got the position since I was majoring in the subject of management.

While pursuing the course of study I met a student in chemical class that was assisting me in the subject. We became very close, and during that period, we had sex once and I became pregnant. I was about three months pregnant when I told my parents and of course, they were very angry because my mom had informed me that this could happen. I had to drop out of school at that point and I remained home until the baby was born. I had a healthy and beautiful little baby girl.

After the birth of my baby girl, my friend was offered a good job as an engineer in New York and accepted it. He later asked me to join him with the baby. I accepted the offer and we lived together for three years, until I found out he was dating a lady in our building. Of course, he lied about it until I caught them together. Without a moment of hesitation, I packed up and went back to live with relatives in his hometown. They were very angry with him and so were my parents, nevertheless, I knew that my daughter and I deserved better, and I was determined to achieve it.

Chapter 2

Employment

After talking with my mother, I explained that I had to earn money so that I could take care of myself and my daughter - it was important that I not be a burden to my parents. She understood and supported my decision and was more than willing to take the baby and care for her while I figured out how I was going to support us. It was a hard decision because I'd have to leave my daughter behind, but I knew she'd be in the best hands and receive the best care. I made the decision to leave my daughter with my mom and return to New York to find employment.

After leaving my daughter with my parents, I returned to Brooklyn and moved in with a couple of friends I had attended school within Greensboro. My roommates were raised up in the church like me, so we attended church every Sunday. They assisted me in finding employment, and I took this time to learn my way around the borough of Brooklyn and travel on the public transportation system. Oh, what experiences indeed!

I was able to land a job as a dietician's aide at the Brooklyn Jewish Hospital located in a section of Brooklyn called Prospect Heights. I enjoyed working at the hospital. The job enlightened me about the variety of diets and meal preparations one had to eat based on the nature of their illness. For example, blue tabs meant the patient was a diabetic, so the meals prepared were to contain no sugar. If the tab was white, then the patient could have a regular meal, but if the tab was pink, then the meals had to be salt free. Although the hours were exhausting, I gained knowledge on how to prepare various meals based on a patient's diet and need. The demands of the job did not allow me to do very much of anything after work except climb into bed and fall asleep almost as soon as my head hit the pillow. For the most part, going to church was my primary outlet and just hanging out with my roommates. They occupied most of my time, and kept me busy, focused and stable, so their presence and friendship alone were good enough for me to wholeheartedly accept and embrace.

I worked at the hospital until the big snow of 1969 also referred to as the Blizzard of '69 which happened in February of that year. I worked for seven weeks without pay, or time off. I particularly remember this time, because my father had passed away and I couldn't get to Greensboro for his funeral. The supervisor called and wanted me to report for duty even thought it was my day off, and when I refused, I was told that I was dismissed. I informed her to send me my paycheck and went on to find a job as a waitress the next day at a restaurant just down the street.

The restaurant owner, who happened to be a sun worshipper, hired me as a waitress. One of his regular customers was the local number runner. He took a liking to me because he said I was clean and respectful, and he was very particular about his food and how it was served. One day he gave me a five-dollar tip and told me to go and buy an apron with pockets. Then he said make sure I turned the apron around so the pockets were out of sight of the restaurant owner. That way I could put my tips in the pocket and the owner wouldn't know I had tip money. He then said, "take your tips and put them in the bank," so I did just that. My relationship and conversations with him served as my first piece of solid financial advice. Why was this so important, well, back then tips were generally coins, rarely a dollar bill, and the owner would count the waitresses' tip change and in return he would give them paper money equal to the change he collected, that way, he never had to give them a raise. When he'd ask me, I would tell him, "No Sir, I'm not receiving any tips," so it turned out that I was the only one who got a raise.

In the Spring of 1969, after working as a waitress, I consistently looked for employment, reading ads in the Daily News, Wall Street Journal and the Amsterdam News, one of New York City's oldest Black newspapers. There were a lot of advertisements for jobs in the newspapers; it was there that I came across a job listing that said, "Community Organizers needed." They were seeking workers for the anti-poverty programs that where plentiful during that time and many applicants were needed, so I applied for the position. I had no knowledge of what the job requirements were, but I was called in for an interview and graciously obliged their invitation to be hired.

Barbara was already working as a job developer and asked various questions about organizers in the area and what made me think I would be the best person for the position. I replied, "If one knows how to organize their home, work and work habits, one would be able to organize anything!" She called me back a couple of days later and told me that I was hired and that she thought I would be the perfect person for the job. I organized block associations, tenant associations, and street fairs and anything else that mobilized the community and provide a positive impact. From time to time, we shared meetings, informing people in the community about employment, tenant organizations and social services. Working in different locations made it easy when we came together for weekly meetings to discuss what was happening in our separate departments. One day Barbara invited me to have lunch at a restaurant nearby. Although I wasn't sure what it meant because I didn't know about gay people, others in the department told me she was gay. I accepted her lunch invitations just the same, and we met every Friday to share lunch or dinner after work.

After four or five months I was promoted to head the home making unit and moved to a church on Greene Avenue where the space was free. The home making unit consisted of training women in the program on "how to" in the community- we knocked on doors and asked families if they needed help with the social services they were entitled to. Those services consisted of obtaining social security, providing assistance in seeking housing, tenant-landlord issues, as well as how families could receive government issued surplus food

16

like cheese and lunch meat items. Although I was never late for work and worked very hard, I was surprised when I got the promotion. However, knowing that an increase in my salary would follow was very rewarding because I could send more money home for my daughter's support.

Bobbi asked to transfer to the same Greene Avenue location since it was near to where she lived. Permission was granted allowing us to see each other daily. I got up early every day just to see her walk to work. It was something about her stride that made me happy. Then it happened, slowly, over time, these little warm and fuzzy feelings, started to seep into my inner self and gradually, I was developing this attraction. She was always smiling; that smile was a killer to me that it just made me tingle inside. I became even more aware of "it" because she started taking one of the secretaries out to lunch every day, and before I knew it and to my

surprise, I felt myself becoming jealous.

Chapter 3

Green Shoes

Bobbi wore a pair of green men's shoes that I thought were ugly. The shoes didn't fit in with the rest of her attire. She wore dresses and skirts and I wanted her to look more feminine. I strongly suggested she get rid of them, so I bought a pair of green shoes that were more feminine looking and to my surprise, she gave up wearing those green masculine shoes (though it's one of my favorite colors now, at that time, those shoes always rubbed me the wrong way.)

At some point I also became very angry about this ongoing lunch situation and confronted her. She asked, "what's wrong with taking someone to lunch?" I replied that since the move, she no longer took or asked me to lunch. The following day when she and the secretary went to lunch, I was ready to fight and tried to push them both down a flight of stairs. Bobbi questioned me as to what was wrong, and I replied, "I don't know"; honestly, I didn't know how to tell her that I was jealous. She told me we would discuss the matter after work. When we were finally able to get together and talk, she informed me that she was gay and, what we used to call back then, a [1]butch. I really didn't understand what gay was, so she explained it to me. The reason she took Liz to lunch was because they were intimate; she liked me a hell of a lot but not to be intimate with me. At this point I tried to understand but I didn't want to accept it.

We did not speak for several weeks, but out of the blue, she asked me to go to lunch again. I refused

---

[1] "Butch is most often a term used to describe a lesbian who exhibits a masculine identity.

even though I wanted to go. Later, I in invited her to come to my place for dinner and she accepted. I asked her what her favorite dish was, and she told me she wasn't choosey and would eat whatever I prepared.

I guess one would say this was our first date. For dinner I prepared smothered pork chops, fresh string beans and mashed potatoes, and cupcakes for dessert. This was the night that I found out that she wasn't fond of string beans, so I had to come up with something quick to make them more "interesting!"

I guess for me, this is where we began.

Chapter 4

Secret Lover

I lived on Dean Street, and she lived on Lafayette Avenue in Brooklyn. We both had furnished kitchenettes which did not have a lot of room. She told me that she didn't want to get involved with me because I was straight. It was at this time - I was dating a man but didn't think much about it. He worked nights and I only saw him during the daytime. I had never been intimate with him and was only with him for the added financial stability he provided. He worked in the Garment District of Manhattan, an area where there were a lot of fashion related businesses, like showrooms, and manufacturers and wholesale sellers. Working in the district he was able to get coats at a discount. He always gave me money on his payday which I needed to send to my mom for the upkeep of my daughter, on top of the extra I was putting in the bank. Bobbi and I had a conversation one day, and she told me it was wrong to use him and that it wasn't a good thing, so after that conversation, I stopped accepting money from him. Instead of him accepting and understanding it, he became very angry and upset.

One night he decided not to go to work and came to my place. That same night, Bobbi and I had planned on being intimate for the first time and almost got caught. It was a good thing I had chain locks on my door because it gave Bobbi a chance to hide in the bathroom. After that, I broke off the relationship with him; I was so glad that I didn't have to lie anymore. I used to tell him that I would be intimate with him, but he just had to wait for the right time. The real truth was I was scared to have a sexual encounter because I didn't want to risk getting pregnant again.

I now was able to make love to her for the first time. We were now able to date on a regular basis. We told people we were sisters, but it was too late to turn back because by then, I felt like I had fallen in love with her. We hooked up and did everything together. She told me that her mother lived in Harlem, had a large apartment and was a barber.   Bobbi's mother did not like her very much, so she lived with her grandmother who raised her. Other family members didn't approve of her lifestyle and said she was just like her mother who was "gay" and living with lots of women. She had her own places of struggle as I did.

Chapter 5

Grandparent Cooking

Bobbi told me her grandmother was such a good cook and made Caribbean "CooCoo" for her with steamed fish. I never had the chance to meet her grandmother because she passed away before I met Bobbi. I did inform her that I could make the same dish for her and that my grandma was a Cherokee Indian born on a reservation in North Carolina. She cooked all her meals outside on a flat grill and never cooked indoors even though she had a stove inside her home. My grandma taught me how to cook before I was seven years old. I guess that's why I have good cooking skills today.

My grandmother had nine children and my mom was her first born. She was a woman who didn't take any mess! She smoked, made and sold home brew, an alcoholic concoction popular in the south. When she passed, she was 102 years old. We traveled to Asheville, North Carolina for her funeral; it was the first one I had ever experienced of our culture and Indian heritage.

Chapter 6

From Commitment to First Christmas

In 1969 we finally decided to move in together. We found a spacious apartment on St. John's Place between Franklin and Bedford Avenue. It had two large bedrooms, a huge kitchen, a large living room with high ceilings a bathroom with an old-fashioned claw foot bathtub. It was large enough to put a bed in it if we chose to! The apartment was on the third floor which was a walk-up, no elevators. We loved that apartment!

Both of us were working and made a pretty good salary, which enabled us to pay the monthly rent. We moved in December since the apartment was vacant near the end of the month. We moved in using shopping carts from our Lafayette and Dean abodes. It was Christmas Eve and we started early in the morning to be in our new place by Christmas Day. The only furnishings we had were two sleeping bags, an ironing board, some pots, pans, and clothing.

After we moved in, we both had errands to run. It was early and I went shopping for groceries and her Christmas gift. She went to Broadway, a big avenue with an assortment of stores to get my gift out of layaway. Afterwards, we prepared for Christmas. Dinner included Cornish hens, cornmeal stuffing, collard greens, sweet potatoes, iced tea, and for dessert, we had ambrosia. We laughed because we ate on paper plates with plastic knives, forks and spoons but that meal was amazing.

Since we had no furniture, we had dinner on the ironing board. We laughed about eating standing up. With no chairs that was the only option we had. Have you ever tried eating on an ironing board? Let me tell you, it's something else! It served as our dining table and the stove top was the added extension for refills. After laughing and discussing our adventures, we found it exciting sleeping and making love in our sleeping bags. If you are in love, nothing seems difficult. That was the best Christmas I had experienced in years.

Our first furniture purchase was a table with four chairs from a used furniture store. Later we purchased a double bed, a coffee table and couch for the living room, and basic household items to complete the furnishings for the apartment. Day by day, it was becoming home.

Chapter 7

Our Daughter

After we settled in at St. John's Place, Bobbi and I discussed sending for my daughter Ursula who was still with my mom in North Carolina. It was time to bring her to New York so she could have closer contact with her dad. It was time to bring her to New York so she could have closer contact with her dad. Although she talked to him every week, she wanted to see him in person. He continued to live in Manhattan with his girlfriend, but it was important to me that she had a stable relationship with both parents. One day my love said to me, "I want you to send for OUR daughter." It really shocked me because she indicated that Ursula was her daughter, too.

She claimed my child as her own. This was the moment when I fell in love with her. I called my mom to tell her we were coming down to get her. This was the time when my mom asked if Bobbi was my dear friend or my lover. I confessed that she was my lover and she told me that she knew and had been aware for a long time. She embraced Bobbi with open arms and so did the rest of my family.

Ursula was turning six and we wanted to enroll her in school. We inquired about schools in the area, and we decided to enroll her in the Village School. She remained there for the first year. Bobbi took her to school every day. Ursula loved the interaction they shared and called her "Auntie B". After the end of the first year, we enrolled her in Catholic School where she and our lives began to flourish.

Chapter 8

From Rental to Ownership

Our lease was about to expire. We started looking at apartments but saw nothing we liked. Bobbi's Aunt Olga knew of a house in the Bedford- Stuyvesant section of Brooklyn that was for sale and told us we should inquire about it.

After we saw the two-family brownstone house and learned of the asking the price, we decided we could not afford it at the time, but Aunt Olga said that she would lend us the money for the down payment, and we could pay her when we got on our feet. Boy, was that a happy day! Bobbi's aunt owned her home for years and told us of the necessary repairs we would have to make before moving in, so we knew what we had to do.

The purchase of 263 Monroe Street was the best thing that happened to us. Bobbi was working in Manhattan, and I was working in the South Bronx. She discussed going back to school which would enable us to be close to home and cut down on traveling. Bobbi decided to enroll and attend Queens College, and I went to Brooklyn College. I had graduated from Medgar Evers College and wanted to complete my Masters in order to teach high school. It was not easy with both of us working full time and Ursula almost ready to graduate from high school. Although it was a challenge, we worked and studied very hard as we were both determined that we could and would all cross the finish line together.

Chapter 9

The Accident

One evening coming home from work, Bobbi was hit by a car driven by an 18-year-old and his girlfriend. They sped off but were chased by men in the neighborhood. Luckily, it occurred two blocks from home. Since we lived only one block from the fire station, they were the first responders. Bobbi was thrown into the air and landed on her right shoulder. She was rushed to Kings County Hospital where they worked on her for hours. Her rotator cuff was damaged, and they kept her there for a couple of weeks until I transferred her to Downstate Medical Center.

She was in constant pain but didn't want to take painkillers. She wanted to come home and be with family instead of staying at Downstate. Upon coming home, we located a doctor at New York Hospital in Manhattan, who stated that the rotator cuff had to be operated on because that was the reason for the constant pain. During the operation, she went into cardiac arrest and was in a coma for a month. They believed she had been given a drug that contained sulfur which may have caused the coma, and at no time was she to have been given any medication containing sulfur. Unable to take a leave of absence, I went to the hospital daily.

Upon dismissal from the hospital, I hired a caregiver as a companion to be with Bobbi until I came home from work. Our life was very difficult during the healing process because she was in constant pain. One evening, after Barb came out of the coma, she told the nurse on duty that she saw visions of angels but she was only able to count to nine as the tenth angel seemed to fade away. The nurse shared that conversation with me; later, I had the opportunity to question Barb about her vision and ask what she thought it meant. She stated that it was possible that the angels were keeping her alive and was a message from God letting her know that she was still alive and still covering her relentlessly.

My honey began to improve and was able to walk without constant pain due to prescribed medication. With the improvement, we agreed to sell our Monroe St. home to make it more convenient for me since I was teaching. We got a good offer for the brownstone and sold it within six months. We found an apartment on Carroll Street. It was very convenient since I was teaching several blocks away at John Jay High School. In the meantime, we were looking for an elevated building. Bobbi had knee surgery and we were living on the third floor of a walk-up building. We needed something that would suit our needs and be comfortable for the both of us.

We both missed the things we used to do such as walking in the rain, being nude at the beach, attending baseball games at Coney Island, making love under the boardwalk, sleeping late Sunday mornings and making candlelight dinners for some of our best friends. Looking for a condo with an elevator was paramount at this stage of the game. Bobbi wanted me to return to school after teaching for twenty-four years so I did. I was able to get a scholarship to Hunter College but only attended for a short time. I had to drop out because of the passing of my mother and young nephew who both died on the same day. We finally found a condo on Second Street and right away she wanted to get married. She wanted to travel to Canada, but I suggested that we wait until it was legal in New York State. The move to

37

Second Street was wonderful. I was free to be a caretaker for my honey, she became more at ease and didn't seem to worry about how we would survive some of the disappointments we had in the past. Despite the challenges, we remained focused on the future.

Chapter 10

Engagement

In 2010 Bobbi gave me an engagement ring at GRIOT Circle, an LGBT community group for Elders of Color that we frequented on a daily basis. Boy, was it a surprise! I will always cherish that memory because even with her bad knee she got down and proposed in front of everyone. She really loved me for being me and I loved her for being the genius she was. She always treated me like a queen and made me the woman I am today. We believed in one another and knew that we would always be together and love one another always.

We waited until July 2011 when Gay marriage became legal in New York State. We were the first couple online to be married when we went to City Hall and applied for our license. We dressed in white for the occasion and after forty-eight years together, we made it legal. The Borough President of Brooklyn hosted more than sixty couples, and we were one of the happily married newlyweds who enjoyed a lovely reception with sparkling water, champagne, cake and a photographer to capture the moments of all the happy couples.

In 2015 The New York Times did a series on Modern Love called "The 36 Questions That Lead to Love" by Daniel Jones. The idea was to see whether total strangers, if asked these questions of each other, could be made to feel closer to each other. Well in 2017, Bobbi and I were fortunate enough to be selected as part of a three-couple revision of that series called 36 Questions That Lead to Love (Again) by Samantha Stark and Bonnie Wertheim. The premise of this revision was to ask these three couples who supposedly knew everything about each other to try out this 36-question concept. We had such a good time and felt truly blessed to have been selected.

Chapter 11

Traveling

In August 2018, we traveled to North Carolina for a planned family reunion. The entire month of July all Bobbi talked about was the reunion trip. We were there for a week and had a wonderful time. Our daughter had not seen many of our relatives but had communicated via phone calls. Bobbi wanted to stay longer but she had doctor appointments. Ursula decided to stay another week and come home later. The family reunion was a joyous occasion for our family so Ursula stayed on to help plan the next one.

My honey enjoyed traveling. She went with several friends to Africa in 1983. She never stopped talking about the things she saw and did. She brought back memories and kept them in a special place. I really wished that I could have gone with her, but working didn't permit it at the time, so I remained at home and took care of business. Two years later, I traveled to China for a month with a group of teachers. I had the opportunity and good fortune to walk a segment of the Great Wall of China to the top. The view was so beautiful, it was like being in heaven. I learned to travel by bus in China, because I wasn't afraid to ask! I stayed in Beijing, traveled to Shanghai, and three other provinces. This was the only time we were separated for any length of time. If there was one thing about us, we were determined to see the world, and we did just that!

Chapter 12

Diagnosis

By late August 2018, I noticed a change in Bobbi's behavior and memory. She would wake up two or three o'clock in the morning, take a shower and get dressed to go outside. I had to stop her before she called for the elevator. She became very agitated, and I had to force her back inside. At this point, I discussed her behavior with my family and several of our close friends. They suggested that I inform her primary doctor. The doctor advised me to start looking for a good nursing home because she was in the early stages of dementia, and I wouldn't be able to take care of her alone.

Looking for a nursing home was a hard task for me. I really didn't want her to go and she didn't want to leave home. After enrolling her in the nursing home, she seemed pleased because I could visit daily. She was liked by staff and didn't give them a hard time. They noted that she was helpful to other patients and wondered if her diagnosis was correct. After the resident doctor re-tested her, he stated the diagnosis was correct. I visited her every day and spent hours with her. She always wanted to come home; I promised her she would come home for Thanksgiving, and she looked forward to that. It was the only consolation I could give her; I couldn't help her, so all I knew to give her was hope and something special to look forward to.

Chapter 13

The Last Goodbye

On October 28, 2018, she asked me to bring her CooCoo and cod fish. When I tried to give it to her, she stated she didn't want it. Her nurse told me she hadn't eaten anything all day and she was concerned. My honey told me she was going "home." Not understanding what she was trying to tell me, I told her I would be taking her home the day before Thanksgiving. She never tried to correct me, but instead just smiled and asked me for a kiss.

It was getting late, and she told me to take a cab and go home. I gave her several kisses and left for home. Later that night, I received a call from the nursing home informing me that she had passed away. On October 29, 2018, my darling left me for the last time. I will never forget how much she loved me and the wonderful fifty-four years we shared together. The magic moments such as making that cup for love making, kisses that quickened me like a wet dog, love making like reaching for the moon and the stars and holding each other all the time at night, love notes left in the bathroom written on gum wrappers, and little surprises left under my dinner plate still flood my mind.

The last goodbye – was it really the last goodbye, or was it a new beginning? Sometimes I realize that she always wanted me above all things to take care of myself instead of others. Did it take her death for me to do just that? I know now that she was right. I'm taking care of me and sometimes others, too.

Bobbi was my gift of love. She was an ardent writer, puzzle solver, dreamer, a lover of life with a strong character and above all, generous and kind. In the end, I would like to warn the angels in heaven to watch out and leave her alone because when I get there, I'm claiming her back. She belongs to me, and I will always love her. An essential part of life is to contribute to the building of friendship, companionship, family, and support, and all that contributes to our well-being.

As a black woman of color, I found it important to reach out and share why I wrote this story and why it's important to me. Before I found out I was gay, that topic was only talked about and discussed in closets or behind closed doors. Now that I understand the importance of who and what I am, it makes it necessary to reach out to others in the hope that they understand love is love. "Gayness" is not the same thing to everyone.

True love is good communication - years of being a devoted mother, wife, teacher, spreader of love, fun loving advocate for people in need and above all, being a truth teller.

Chapter 14

Recipe for Unconditional Love

After listening to other younger generations, I find it necessary to share my gay life with others. It may aid them in their relationship.

A Recipe for Unconditional Love

7 pounds of Communication

12 pounds of Understanding

4 pounds of Forgiving

20 pounds each of Hugs and Kisses

1 large Jar of Honey

1 bottle of Red Wine

(Mix all the above ingredients)

"If you remember me, then I don't care if everyone else forgets.

-Haruki Murakami

Connect with the Author
Geraldine Whitsett

Geraldine (<u>Gerri</u>) Whitsett was born on June 4, 1935, to the late Robert and Elizabeth Whitsett, and her arrival was shaped by God. Her father was employed by Cone Mills, a textile mill. He always told his children that he attended high school for only three days! Whitsett learned that it was true, as she had the opportunity to meet his teacher, but it was her mother who taught her father to read. Her mother's mother was full blooded Cherokee and had grown up on a reservation in Asheville, North Carolina, but married a man from Barbados, West Indies and moved to the great state of South Carolina.

Whitsett grew up in Greensboro, North Carolina, and was the oldest of eight children - three brothers and four sisters, whom she loved dearly. Her family was a church going family and placed a high value on education.

Geraldine Whitsett attended and proudly graduated from James B. Dudley High School. She fondly remembers always telling her siblings that one day she would be paid to be a teacher, and those words would one day come to pass. She attended North Carolina Agricultural and Technical State University (A&T) for two years before dropping out for financial reasons, but not before participating in the history-making lunch counter sit-in at the Woolworth's discount department store in Greensboro. During that time, Woolworth's allowed blacks to shop, but they were not allowed to eat at the lunch counter. It was February 1960 when she answered a call for participants from flyers advertised around the campus. Within weeks, the protests spread to all the Woolworth's locations throughout the south and by July, 1960 the Woolworth chain agreed to desegregate all of their lunch counters within the company.

After dropping out of A&T, Whitsett found employment with the United Cab Company where she worked as a dispatcher; she then moved on to work at Moses Cone Hospital as a "tray girl".

Wanting more for herself, Whitsett eventually moved to New York where she found employment with the Office of Economic Opportunity Agency where she worked with the war on poverty programs created during the Johnson Administration. Returning back to school, she graduated from Medgar Evers College, of the City University of New York with a B.A. degree in Early Childhood Education, then went on to Brooklyn College where she earned a Master's in Guidance and Counseling. While employed by the New York City Board of Education, she taught for twenty-four years, as a teacher, earning the Teacher of the Year award for three consecutive years, guidance counselor and dean. She traveled throughout the Caribbean and four provinces in China before retiring from the Board of Education.

Today, she enjoys working with her hands designing God's Eye crafts, a symbol of the power of seeing and understanding unseen things, cooking and creating menus.

Made in the USA
Middletown, DE
19 June 2023

32838099R00038